THE SUPERNATURAL POWER OF FAITH

"For verily I say unto you, That whosoever shall say unto this mountain, Be thou removed, and be thou cast into the sea; and shall not doubt in his heart, but shall believe that those things which he saith shall come to pass; he shall have whatsoever he saith."

Mark 11:23

By
Franklin N Abazie

The Supernatural Power of Faith

Just as you'll never understand the mystery of life forming in a pregnant woman, So you'll never understand the mystery at work in all that God does. **Ecll11:5MSG**

COPYRIGHT@ 2016 BY Franklin N Abazie

ISBN978-1-94513311-4

All right reserved. This book or any portion thereof may not be reproduced or used in any manner whatsoever without the express written permission of the publisher, except for the use of brief quotations in a book review. All Bible quotes are from King James Version and others as noted.

Published by: F N ABAZIE PUBLISHING HOUSE- a.k.a Empowerment Bookstore.

Psalms 26:7 That I may publish with the voice of thanksgiving and tell of all thy wondrous works.

To order additional copies, wholesales or booking: Call the Church office 973-372-7518, or call Empowerment Bookstore Hotline 973-393-8518

Worship address: 343 Sanford Avenue Newark New Jersey 07106

Administrative Head Office address: 33 Schley Street Newark New Jersey 07112 Email:pastorfranknto@yahoo.com

Website www.fnabaziehealingministries.org

Publishing House: www.fnabaziepublishinghouse.org

This book is a production of F N Abazie Publishing House. A publication Arms of Miracle of God Ministries 2016 First Edition

CONTENTS

THE MANDATE OF THE COMMISSION............iv

ARMS OF THE COMMISSION...............................v

INTRODUCTION……………………….....………vi

CHAPTER 1

1. The Desperate Faith 25

CHAPTER 2

2. The Prevailing Faith..56

CHAPTER 3

3. The Enduring Faith..92

CHAPTER 4

4. Prayer of Salvation...122

CHAPTER 5

5. About the Author..132

THE MANDATE OF THE COMMISSION

"The moment is due to impact your world through the revival of the healing & miracle ministry of Jesus Christ of Nazareth. "I am sending you to restore health unto thee and I will heal thee of thy wounds, said the Lord of Host."

ARMS OF THE COMMISSION

1) F N Abazie Ministries-Miracle of God Ministries (Miracle Chapel Intl)

2) F N Abazie TV Ministries: Global Television Ministry Outreach.

3) F N Abazie Radio Ministries: Radio Broadcasting Outreach.

4) F N Abazie Publishing House: Book Publication.

5) F N Abazie Bible School: also called Word of Healing Bible School (W.O.H.B.S)

6) F N Abazie Evangelistic Ass: Miracle of God Ministries: Global Crusade

7) Empowerment Bookstore: Book distribution.

8) F N Abazie Helping Hands: Meeting the help of the needy world wide

9) F N Abazie Disaster Recovery Mission: Global Disaster Recovery.

10) F N Abazie Prison Ministry: Prison Ministry for all convicts "Second chance"

Some of our ministry arms are waiting the appointed time to commence.

INTRODUCTION

"Nevertheless, when the Son of man cometh, shall he find faith on the earth?"
Luke18:8

For the most part, I decided to put this book together because Jesus Christ is looking for faith in us all. We are told that without faith it is impossible to please Him. Contrary to all the prosperity theology we hear today, God is looking for faith in our heart. We are saved by grace but through faith in Jesus Christ our Lord.

"For by grace are ye saved through faith; and that not of yourselves: it is the gift of God:" **Ephesians2:8**

This book the supernatural power of faith is a book that will not only enlighten and encourage our faith in Christ Jesus, but will convict us to repent of our sinful ways and motivate us to make higher moves in life.It is my desire to introduce this book to all who believe in the validity of the power of God.

In this challenging times, most people are crying for the manifestation of the supernatural power of God. In my own opinion nothing happens unless we have faith in God. And Faith in God means believing God, remaining optimistic and positive in life. As a man of faith I believe this small book will make a great difference in our own lives. We are told that the just shall live by faith.

The case study in this book is faith in God. That is all it takes to please God. But faith in God does not work unless we develop love.

"For faith works by love." **gal 5:6.**

In this book you will understand how to apply action to our spoken words, we will learn how to remain calm in the midst of prevailing difficulties, challenges, and impossibilities in life.

We have the privilege to make a choice in life. No man can interpret and chose for us in life.

Among the noble choices we make in life is a choice to have faith in God and to remain faithful to the calling of God.

This small book will encourage and give hope to anyone in pursuit of the things of God. I have no doubt that this book will help build you faith in God.

It is written *"For whatsoever is born of God overcometh the world: and this is the victory that overcometh the world, even our faith."* **1John5:5.**

What we call faith is not faith unless there is a corresponding action to back up our heart desire. I pray we all take positive steps in life as we develop supernatural faith in God. We must make faith an everyday thing.

Remember……..

"……….. for whatsoever is not of faith is sin."
Romans14:23

HIS DESTINY WAS THE CROSS….

HIS PURPOSE WAS LOVE…..

HIS REASON WAS YOU….

"For whatsoever is born of God overcometh the world: and this is the victory that overcometh the world, even our faith."

1John5:4

Supernatural faith prayer points

"For every one that asketh receiveth; and he that seeketh findeth; and to him that knocketh it shall be opened."
Mathew 7:8

Power of God frustrate and disappoint, every one that is against my life and family, in the name of Jesus.

Heavenly Father Lord destroy every demonic networks and traps against my progress in life in the name of Jesus.

Hand of God, destroy every demonic projection and curses against my life and destiny in the name of Jesus.

Every spell and curses pronounced against my destiny, break, in the name of Jesus.

Hand of God cage every power militating against my rising in life, in the name of Jesus.

Power of God silent every voice raising a counter motion against my elevation, in the mighty name of Jesus.

Blood of Jesus neutralize every spirit of Balaam hired to hinder my life, ministry, and career, the name of Jesus.

Fire of God destroy every curse that I have brought into my life through ignorance and disobedience, break by fire, in the name of Jesus.

Ancient of day destroy every power harassing my ministry in the name of Jesus.

Father God deliver me from invincible forces militating against my life and destiny.

Power of God frustrate every coven and demonic network, designed to frustrate and hinder my success in life, in the name of Jesus.

I dismantle every strong hold designed to imprison my talent in the mighty name of Jesus.

I reject every cycle of frustration, in the name of Jesus.

Power of God paralyze every agent assigned to frustrate my life in the name of Jesus.

Finger of God, grant me supernatural speed against all my contenders in the name of Jesus.

By the blood of Jesus, I destroy every familiar spirit caging my life and career.

Fire of God arrest every demonic agents, assigned to police my destiny and marriage.

By the blood of Jesus, I proclaim no weapon fashioned against me shall ever prosper.

Holy Spirit of God break me through and forward in life in the mighty name of Jesus.

God, smash me and renew my strength, in the name of Jesus.

Father Lord grant me strength and power in the name of Jesus

O Lord, liberate my spirit to follow the leading of the Holy Spirit

Holy Spirit, teach me to pray through problems instead of praying about, it in the name of Jesus.

Father Lord, deliver me from the false accusation in life, in the name of Jesus

By the blood of Jesus, every evil spiritual padlock and evil chain hindering my success, be roasted, in the name of Jesus.

By the blood of Jesus I rebuke every spirit of spiritual deafness and blindness in my life, in the name of Jesus.

Father Lord, empower me to dominate the enemy of my destiny in the name of Jesus.

Jesus Christ of Nazareth, heal my infirmities in the name of Jesus

Lord, anoint my eyes and my ears that they may see and hear wondrous things from heaven.

Father Lord, anoint me with power and authority to dominate all my enemies in the name of Jesus.

Fire of God roast every giant rising up against my life and career.

Holy Spirit of God destroy all my oppressors in the name of Jesus.

Angels of good new, bring my good news to me in the mighty name of Jesus.

Every strong man holding me down, lose your hold now in the name of Jesus.

I nullify every demonic prediction over my life in the name of Jesus.

By the blood of Jesus, I flush out every polluted deposit of the enemy in my life.

Angels of good new, bring my good news to me in the mighty name of Jesus.

Every strong man holding me down, lose your hold now in the name of Jesus.

I nullify every demonic prediction over my life in the name of Jesus.

By the blood of Jesus, I flush out every polluted deposit of the enemy in my life.

By the blood of Jesus, I paralyze every enemy of my promotion in the name of Jesus.

Father Lord, destroy any power tormenting my life that is not from you.

Holy Ghost fire, ignite the fire of revival in my life.

By the blood of Jesus, I declare victory over every conflicting trial

By the Blood of Jesus, I command the arrest of every demonic spirit, militating against my life

By the blood of Jesus, I proclaimed the blood of Jesus, over every device of the enemy.

By the blood of Jesus, I revoke stagnation and hardship over my life in the name of Jesus.

Holy Ghost fire, destroy every satanic arrangement in my life, in the name of Jesus.

HOW TO PROVOKE SPIRITUAL BLESSING

"And seeing the multitudes, he went up into a mountain: and when he was set, his disciples came unto him:

And he opened his mouth, and taught them, saying,

Blessed are the poor in spirit: for theirs is the kingdom of heaven.

Blessed are they that mourn: for they shall be comforted.

Blessed are the meek: for they shall inherit the earth.

Blessed are they which do hunger and thirst after righteousness: for they shall be filled.

Blessed are the merciful: for they shall obtain mercy.

Blessed are the pure in heart: for they shall see God.

Blessed are the peacemakers: for they shall be called the children of God.

Blessed are they which are persecuted for righteousness' sake: for theirs is the kingdom of heaven.

Blessed are ye, when men shall revile you, and persecute you, and shall say all manner of evil against you falsely, for my sake.

Rejoice, and be exceeding glad: for great is your reward in heaven: for so persecuted they the prophets which were before you."

Mathew5:1-12

THE LAW OF RECEIVING IS HIDDEN IN GIVING
"To give we must love"

"For God so loved the world that he gave his only begotten Son, that whosoever believeth in him should not perish, but have everlasting life."

"To receive, we must give,"

It is written *"Give, and it shall be given unto you; good measure, pressed down, and shaken together, and running over, shall men give into your bosom. For with the same measure that ye mete withal it shall be measured to you again."* **Luke6:38.**

If we must receive in life, we must become givers ourselves. Jesus said it is more blessing to give than to receive. Every time we give, we position our life for power and for next level.

"But as many as received him, to them gave he power to become the sons of God, even to them that believe on his name:"
John1:12

How do I give?

1) We give cheerfully to God. **2cor9:7**

2) We give willingly to God. **1cor9:17, exodus 35:5-22**

3) We give righteously to God. **Mal3:3**.

4) We give in faith to God. **Eccl11:1**

5) We give in love to God. **1King3:3, John3:16**

6) We give liberally to God. **Proverb11:25, proverb28:27**

7) We give to God for health and longlife. **Psalm41:1-3, Ps91:16**

8) We give to support the kingdom of God. **Mathew.6:33**

9) We give our best, not left over. **Mal1:6-8, 2sam24:24**

----WHEN YOU ARE ALONE MIND YOUR THAUGHTS---

Whenever you are lonely always make efforts to occupy you mind with positive thoughts. As long as you are optimistic the prevailing challenges will eventually take a positive shape in your favor.

Reading positive new like the bible is a recommended way to stay positive.

Stay away from the television, the radio station unless you turn into a spirit lifting song channel otherwise the new media is designed to depressed you with wrong and bad new and misleading information.

-WHEN WE ARE WITH OUR FRIENDS WE MUST CONTROL OUR TONGUE-

"Even so the tongue is a little member, and boasteth great things. Behold, how great a matter a little fire kindleth!

And the tongue is a fire, a world of iniquity: so is the tongue among our members, that it defileth the whole body, and setteth on fire the course of nature; and it is set on fire of hell."
James3:5-6

      I tell you the truth, your tongue is power more than you understand it. We are told that life and death is in the power of the tongue. We must therefore guide our tongue diligently against every rude, crude, or defiling words. We create and destroy with our tongue we must hence forth speak life and good concerning our life and concerning others around us. If you must do will in the faith and in life, you must guide your tongue diligently.

---WHEN WE ARE ANGRY WE MUST CONTROL OUR EMOTIONS---

"Be ye angry, and sin not: let not the sun go down upon your wrath:" **Ephesians4:26**

"Be not hasty in thy spirit to be angry: for anger resteth in the bosom of fools." **Eccl7:9**

The bible says be angry but sin not, So there is nothing wrong with getting angry, there is only a problem with our emotions and the after effect of our frame of mind. We must be cool tempered even in critical time of severe emotional challenges.

In my own understanding every hardship has an expiring date, every difficulty have a time to come to an end. Jesus said for the things concerning me have an end.

"……for the things concerning me have an end." **Luke22:37.**

As long as we can endure hardship and prevailing times, God will prove himself mighty in our lives.

"For his anger endureth but a moment; in his favour is life: weeping may endure for a night, but joy cometh in the morning" **Psalms30:5**

"For our light affliction, which is but for a moment, worketh for us a far more exceeding and eternal weight of glory;" **2cor4:17**

".....for the Egyptians whom ye have seen to day, ye shall see them again no more for ever." **Exodus14:13.**

I encourage you to key into these scriptures above and be dominate every obstacle.

CHAPTER 1
The Desperate Faith

"And blessed is she that believed: for there shall be a performance of those things which were told her from the Lord."
Luke1:45

Unless we understand the word "desperate", it will be difficult to understand the entire title to this chapter together," Desperate faith". The word desperate means a state of despair, typically one that results in rash or extreme behavior. This I mean -the condition of being desperate.

Recklessness arising from despair. Have you ever been late and desperate to catch up with your flight departure time? That is what we mean in a nut shell about desperate faith.

In our life time there comes a season or moment when life prevailing circumstances, obstacles, and hindrances provoke us to be desperate for one thing or the other.

In my own words desperate times requires desperate faith in God to confront it. Without desperate faith in God we end up in despair and hopelessness in life.

It is written *"For to him that is joined to all the living there is hope: for a living dog is better than a dead lion."* **Eccl9:4.**

We have to be desperately seeking the help of God in prayers and fasting, supplication, in thanksgiving, and intercession for desperate faith to work. Desperate faith in God gives us confidence that our God will do something supernatural for us at the appointed time.

Even when we suffer set back and any form of defeat we are always hopeful because our God will still lift us up out again.

Chapter 1 - The Desperate Faith

" What do ye imagine against the Lord? he will make an utter end: affliction shall not rise up the second time."
Nahum1:9

"For there is hope of a tree, if it be cut down, that it will sprout again, and that the tender branch thereof will not cease.
Job14:8

As believers we hope even at the last minute that God will rise up and alleviate us from any prevailing predicament prevailing against us in life.

Although we all hope in God every man/woman of faith whose faith have not been tested cannot be trusted. God allows us to experience desperate situation so that he will validate his covenant.

So many of us claim we have faith in God but really what we have is just a mere word of confession from our lip. There is nothing that look like faith in our acclaimed proclamation.

It is written without faith we cannot please God. Prevailing circumstances does not obey fasting and begging in prayers. Every time circumstances prevailed in our lives, we must pull out desperate faith in God to overcome.

What is a desperate Faith?

Jesus established this truth; in our life time there will be prevailing challenges and obstacles opposing us. Mountains and limit that we must conquer and break the limitation. Note that just because we are save and received the free gift of salvation does not exempt us from trials and tribulations in life.

"These things I have spoken unto you, that in me ye might have peace. In the world ye shall have tribulation: but be of good cheer; I have overcome the world." **John16:33**.

Chapter 1 - The Desperate Faith

We must all take desperate measures in desperate times in our lives.

Have you ever find yourself in a desperate situation, or under a severe financial pressure or challenge? Desperate circumstances needs desperate faith in God to subdue it. So many of us have quite often experienced prevailing circumstances that demanded desperate faith in God to overcome it.

Queen Esther who was desperate to save the Jewish people was determined to even die. That is desperate faith in God in display.

Queen Esther said…..

"Go, gather together all the Jews that are present in Shushan, and fast ye for me, and neither eat nor drink three days, night or day: I also and my maidens will fast likewise; and so I will go unto the King, which is not according to the law: and if I perish, I perish."

Esther 4:16

The story of peter is a typical example of desperate faith in God.

"And Peter answered him and said, Lord, if it be thou, bid me come unto thee on the water. And he said, Come. And when Peter was come down out of the ship, he walked on the water, to go to Jesus.

But when he saw the wind boisterous, he was afraid; and beginning to sink, he cried, saying, Lord, save me. And immediately Jesus stretched forth his hand, and caught him, and said unto him, O thou of little faith, wherefore didst thou doubt?" **Mathew 14:28-31**

Apostle Peter who was desperate for Jesus to save him in the above scripture, is the same man that denied Jesus three times before cook crow, during Jesus trials and arrest.

Often we claim we have faith in God but when prevailing circumstances, and challenges pose against us as a mountain we easily succumb to defeat.

Chapter 1 - The Desperate Faith

Desperate faith means making the word of God a law in our life.

This I mean believing in God without any reservation, hope and expectation from any other mortal being or source. In my own understanding it takes faith to enjoy God's presence in our life. The more we increase our faith in God, the more of God's presence and the more of God power for the release of His Signs, and wonder upon our lives.

APOSTLE PAUL

Apostle Paul was so desperate that he was not only ready to go to jail but also to die if that what it will take for him to accomplish his mission.

" And when he was come unto us, he took Paul's girdle, and bound his own hands and feet, and said, Thus saith the Holy Ghost, So shall the Jews at Jerusalem bind the man that owneth this girdle, and shall deliver

him into the hands of the Gentiles. And when we heard these things, both we, and they of that place, besought him not to go up to Jerusalem.

Then Paul answered, What mean ye to weep and to break mine heart? for I am ready not to be bound only, but also to die at Jerusalem for the name of the Lord Jesus." **Acts21:11-13.**

Apostle Paul made so much impact especially in the New Testament because he was a man of desperate faith in God.

One time he said, *"……for I know whom I have believed, and am persuaded that he is able to keep that which I have committed unto him against that day."* **2timothy1:12**

I recommend you develop desperate faith in God. A faith that does not seek any alternative but the will of God to prevail. A faith developed from the heart for conquest and dominion in life.

Chapter 1 - The Desperate Faith

We all must grow in faith and use our faith in God to overcome the wicked devil.

" We know that whosoever is born of God sinneth not; but he that is begotten of God keepeth himself, and that wicked one toucheth him not." **1John5:18**

HOW DO WE DEVELOP FAITH IN GOD?

---- Develop God's faith in our heart----

It is written *"Jesus said unto him, Thou shalt love the Lord thy God with all thy heart, and with all thy soul, and with all thy mind. This is the first and great commandment. And the second is like unto it, Thou shalt love thy neighbour as thyself. On these two commandments hang all the law and the prophets."*

Mathew22:37-40.

Simply defined, we develop faith in God by spreading the love of God in our heart.

"And hope maketh not ashamed; because the love of God is shed abroad in our hearts by the Holy Ghost which is given unto us." **Romans5:5.**

Faith does not work without love.

Remember…

"but faith which worketh by love." **Gal5:6**

"And Jesus answering saith unto them, Have faith in God." **Mark11:22.**

We must embrace faith from our inner conscience to God. The supernatural power of God flows out of our spirit and it affects our heart- that is, it affects the way we think, feel, and see things around us in life. This have power to divert and hinder our God given blessing and inheritance.

Chapter 1 - The Desperate Faith

Faith in God defies all logic and secular knowledge of man. Faith in God provokes the natural things to come into compliance and in alignment with the will of God. Anyone who inhabits bitterness and have no love cannot experience faith in spiritual things.

Faith works by love therefore we must confess and clean our heart from all unrighteousness.

" Not for that we have dominion over your faith, but are helpers of your joy: for by faith ye stand." **2cor1:24**

"For we walk by faith, not by sight:" **2cor5:7**

Remember….

"While we look not at the things which are seen, but at the things which are not seen: for the things which are seen are temporal; but the things which are not seen are eternal." **2cor4:18.**

Everything we see, feel, and touch today is temporary, this I mean everything is subject to change at any time.

"For his anger endureth but a moment; in his favour is life: weeping may endure for a night, but joy cometh in the morning." **Psalms30:6**

For us to walk by faith, we must be optimistic and positive about the outcome of any prevailing challenges opposing us in life. We must be discipline and determined never to give up the fight of faith. Life will only deliver to us what we are willing to fight for.

WE MUST PUT ACTION TO OUR FAITH

Have you ever heard these phrase, "action speak louder than words?" Our God is a God of knowledge, and by him actions are weighed.

Chapter 1 - The Desperate Faith

God is a spirit look for actions in our lives. A married couple may pray about having children, but unless they consummate the marriage and celebrate their love by reproduction- this I mean putting action in their desires, they will never have a child.

Perhaps you are a business owner, an apprentice, or you work for someone unless we take action in life we will never change level.

Taking action in life is a demonstration of our professed faith in our Lord Jesus Christ. A lot of us fool ourselves, by confessing the faith without a corresponding action in our lives to match what we are saying and what we believe.

A lot of us claim to have faith in God, we desire so-many things and make so much demand from God; but do not put an action plan to back our vision or desires.

Our faith is dead unless there is a corresponding action plan, genuinely geared towards the spoken word in faith.

Action oriented believers are faithful men and women. We must always take action concerning our heart desire because God is too faithful to fail us in life.

It is written *"Faithful is he that calleth you, who also will do it."* **1theo5:24**

We must always have an active action plan for actualize our desired goal and desires.

Apostle Paul said *"..... for I know whom I have believed, and am persuaded that he is able to keep that which I have committed unto him against that day."* **2timothy1:12.**

As long as we take corresponding action in life, our God is obligated to back us up. The Omnipotent God is too faithful to fail us in life.

Chapter 1 - The Desperate Faith

Remember……………..

"…………There hath not failed one word of all his good promise, which he promised by the hand of Moses his servant." **1King8:56.**

WE MUST PLAN OUR LIFE

If we fail to plan we have planned to fail one man said. Unless we make a plan we will not know how and where to take the corresponding action in life. There is greatness in planning. Our life will remain plain without a plan and without an action pattern we will remain battered in life.

It is written *"For which of you, intending to build a tower, sitteth not down first, and counteth the cost, whether he have sufficient to finish it?"* **Luke14:28.**

Success in life is a function of plan. I encourage you today; you must plan your life on a daily bases, monthly bases and yearly bases. Planning is the gateway to a glorious future in life.

As we move over to the next chapter, keep this book besides you for ten minutes and revisit your plan with God in prayers.

WHAT ARE THE BENEFITS OF DESPERATE FAITH IN GOD?

-We overcome by desperate faith in God-

Unless we are determined to overcome the wicked one, he always have power to sway us. Remember Satan is the god of this world.

It is written *"In whom the god of this world hath blinded the minds of them which believe not, lest the light of the glorious gospel of Christ, who is the image of God, should shine unto them."* **2cor4:4**

----We win by desperate faith in God----

Every champion must fight a winning battle. We deploy desperate faith in God to confront the enemy and win our life battle that must be overcome for our rising in life.

Chapter 1 - The Desperate Faith

I encourage you to be determined to overcome the devil with all his tricks and assaults in Jesus Mighty Name.

-We prove our sincerity of love for Christ-

Most church folks claim we love God, but truly it's just a lip talk. How many of us are ready to die for Christ Jesus. We must take action in life if we claim we love God. And taking action means deploying desperate faith and making a move.

Queen Esther said if I perish, I perish. Desperate faith in God is a faith mystery developed out of conviction and love. Unless we are convicted and love God desperate faith in God will not work for us.

The three Hebrew boys were convinced and convicted from the heart that no matter what happened to them, that God was able to deliver them from the hand of the wicked King.

"Shadrach, Meshach, and Abednego, answered and said to the king, O Nebuchadnezzar, we are not careful to answer thee in this matter. If it be so, our God whom we serve is able to deliver us from the burning fiery furnace, and he will deliver us out of thine hand, O king." **Daniel 3:16-17.**

It is my desire for you to always believe God can do all thing? **See Jer32:27, Mathew19:26, Mark 10:27, and luke1:37**

Is there anything you're going through in life that makes you wonder if God is able to handle it? It will only take your faith in God to see or witness the miracle that you desire.

There are few accounts in the Bible where God declared that nothing is too difficult for Him.

Chapter 1 - The Desperate Faith

---When Confronting Abraham about Sarah's Laughter and Unbelief----

Abraham was entertaining three persons who appeared to him (Angels appearing in human form) and they gave him the promise of having a son. Abraham and Sarah were advanced in age and way past child bearing age.

From the bible perspective, I believe she had already gone through menopause.

It was impossible for them to have a child in the natural. Sarah heard the promise from her tent door and laughed. And the Lord said, *"Is anything too difficult for the LORD"* **(Genesis 18:14)**

Is there something you feel God has promised you that seems impossible? It may be so disappointed that if you told someone they would laugh.

God's question for you today is the same question he asked Abraham, *"Is anything too difficult for the LORD"* **(Genesis 18:14)**

----In Relation to God's Purposes Being Fulfilled----

In the midst of all his trouble, trials and testing's, Job said, *"I know that You can do everything, and that no purpose of Yours can be withheld from You"* **(Job 42:2).**

What are you presently going through? What trial or time of testing are you confronted with? I believe, God want to do something new for you, but do you believe God can do anything, and that nothing can thwart His purposes from being fulfilled?

It's one thing to believe in God's ability when all is well, but quite another thing to believe the hand of God when there is virtually no hope.

Chapter 1 - The Desperate Faith

Job is our typical example, you've lost everything and your world is falling apart. Believe me and believe God. All it takes is faith for God to put you together and bless your life once again.

-----When Comparing His Ability to His Creative Power-----

In contemplating the creation of the universe, Jeremiah wrote, *"Ah Lord GOD! Behold, You have made the heavens and the earth by Your great power and by Your outstretched arm! Nothing is too difficult for You"* **(Jeremiah 32:17).**

If God was able to create the heavens and the earth with His spoken Word, could there possibly be anything that is to hard for Him?

When Dealing with Mary's Astonishment that She Would Give Birth to the Son of God

Mary was engaged to be married, and unlike most today, she had never slept with her fiancé. An angel appeared to her, telling her she was going to give birth to a son. In her astonishment she said, *"How can this be, since I am a virgin"* **(Luke 1:34)**

The Angel's response was, *"The Holy Spirit will come upon you, and the power of the Most High will overshadow you; and for that reason the holy Child shall be called the Son of God. For nothing will be impossible with God"* **(Luke 1:35 and 37).**

I love Mary's response. It was one of faith. *"Behold the handmaid of the Lord; be it unto me according to thy word"* **(Luke 1:38).**

Let's respond to His promises in faith like this young women did.

Chapter 1 - The Desperate Faith

---When Dealing with the Impossibility of Man to Save Himself---

Jesus had just finished ministering to the rich young ruler, who said he had kept all the commandments from his youth. Jesus told him he lacked one thing,

"If thou wilt be perfect, go and sell all that thou hast, and give to the poor, and thou shalt have treasure in heaven: and come and follow me. But when the young man heard that saying, he went away sorrowful: for he had great possessions" **(Matthew 19:21-22).**

Jesus went on to tell his disciples it was easier for a camel to pass through the eye of a needle than for a rich man to enter the kingdom of God. The disciples responded, *"Who then can be saved? But Jesus looked at them and said, "With men this is impossible, but with God all things are possible"* **(Matthew 19:25-26).**

God is omnipotent and is able to do anything. No matter what you are going through or facing today, our God is able! It may seem impossible in the natural, but let me assure you on the authority of God's Word, He is able.

I'm personally going through something right now that seems impossible. There have been times that the situation seemed dealt with, but the same thing continues to raise it's ugly head over and over again.

I'm reminded of something I read in Dake's Annotated Bible.

"All men (Christians) believe God can do anything, but few believe He will."

Will we dare to believe God is not only able to work in our situation but that he will?

Chapter 1 - The Desperate Faith

God is Able to:

God is Able to Save

"Wherefore He is able also to save them to the uttermost that come unto God by Him, seeing He ever lives to make intercession for them" **(Hebrews 7:25)**.

The word uttermost in the King James Version can also be translated, completely and forever.

God is able to save us completely and forever. No matter how messed up you are, or how far you've fallen into sin, God is able to save you completely and forever if you will surrender to Him with all your heart.

God is Able to Deliver Us

The three Hebrew children expressed confidence in God's ability and said, *"our God whom we serve is able to deliver us from the burning fiery furnace, and He will deliver us from your hand, O king"* **(Daniel 3:17)**.

They not only expressed faith in God's ability, but that He would deliver them – "He will deliver us".

God is able to deliver us from sin and peril. *"He shall save his people from their sins"*

(Matthew 1:21).

"And so all Israel shall be saved: as it is written, There shall come out of Zion the Deliverer, and shall turn away ungodliness from Jacob: For this is my covenant unto them, when I shall take away their sins" **(Romans 11:26-27 KJV).**

Jesus said, *"The Spirit of the Lord is upon me, because he hath anointed me to preach the gospel to the poor; he hath sent me to heal the brokenhearted, to preach deliverance to the captives, and recovering of sight to the blind, to set at liberty them that are bruised"*

(Luke 4:18).

Chapter 1 - The Desperate Faith

God is Able to Heal

"The blind men came to him: and Jesus saith unto them, Believe ye that I am able to do this? They said unto him, Yea, Lord" **(Matthew 9:28).**

Jesus is still in the healing business. He is able to heal us from whatever ails us. Whether we are suffering physically, emotionally, from depression, mentally, mental illness or from some sin that has us in it's grip. God is able to heal us.

The key is, will we let Him? Jesus said to a lame man, *"Do you wish to get well"* (**John 5:6**) Do we really want to be made well? That was Jesus' condition of healing and deliverance.

Frequently, people hate their illness and sin, but they do not really want to be made whole.

For those whose lives have thrown them into intense bondage, there is something that is necessary on your part. You must give your life to Jesus. It's usually the case of those who have sold out to sin that they must fully surrender to Christ with all their heart. It's then that salvation, deliverance and complete wholeness comes into their life.

On the authority of God's Word, God is still in the business of saving, delivering and healing.

God is Able to Keep Us from Falling

"Now unto him that is able to keep you from falling, and to present you faultless before the presence of his glory with exceeding joy" **(Jude 24)**

Once He has delivered us, God is more than able to keep us from falling into the same sins and traps that have held us in their grip. If we will cling to and hold onto Him, He will sustain us and keep us from stumbling.

Chapter 1 - The Desperate Faith

God is Able to Keep Us from Temptation

"There hath no temptation taken you but such as is common to man: but God is faithful, who will not suffer you to be tempted above that ye are able; but will with the temptation also make a way to escape, that ye may be able to bear it" **(1 Corinthians 10:13)**

When we are facing temptation on every front, God is able to deliver us and will provide a way of escape. We must, however, walk through the escape route He provides.

God is Able to Provide

"God is able to make all grace abound toward you; that ye, always having all sufficiency in all things, may abound to every good work" **(2 Corinthians 9:8).**

The context of this verse is referring to financial provision. The key is, God is able to bless us financially so we can abound to every good work – and not just lavish it upon ourselves.

"There are some who are reading these words that God has blessed abundantly. If you want to continue in His blessing, you must find an outlet for the blessings you have received. Find a reputable ministry and sow into it. God has blessed you for that very purpose, in order that you might be a blessing"

(Genesis 12:2).

If you don't use some of your abundance to abound to every good work, God may take away that which you have.

"For unto every one that hath shall be given, and he shall have abundance: but from him that hath not shall be taken away even that which he hath" **(Matthew 25:29).**

In closing, let me share a few encouraging verses from God's Word:

Chapter 1 - The Desperate Faith

"Now unto Him who is able to do exceeding abundantly above all that we ask or think, according to the power that worketh in us"
(Ephesians 3:20).

"The eyes of the LORD move to and fro throughout the earth that He may strongly support those whose heart is completely his"
(2 Chronicles 16:9).

CHAPTER 2
The Prevailing Faith

"If it be so, our God whom we serve is able to deliver us from the burning fiery furnace, and he will deliver us out of thine hand, O king." **Daniel 3:17**

"My God hath sent his angel, and hath shut the lions' mouths, that they have not hurt me: forasmuch as before him innocency was found in me; and also before thee, O king, have I done no hurt." **Daniel 6:22**

Again, unless we understand the word "prevail", it will be touch for me to explain prevailing faith to you. In my own simple definition to prevail means-- To overcome; to gain the victory or superiority; to gain the advantage.

To prevail or prove more powerful than opposing forces; be victorious. For example David prevailed over the Philistine with a sling and with a stone.

Chapter 2 - The Prevailing Faith

Life is full of arising circumstances that we must overcome and prevail if we must make an impact in our generation.

Have you ever experience a prevailing obstacle that have tarried for a long time? Unless we develop strong prevailing faith in times of prevailing circumstances, we will succumb to the will of the opposition.

The fact that we are saved or confess Jesus as Lord does not exempt us from the challenges of life. Let's face it, on a daily bases every one of us is faced with daily prevailing challenges, obstacles, and prevailing difficulties in life.

Unless we confront and conquer it now, it have potentials and power to prevail above us. Remember the devil was called a serpent in genesis chapter three verse fourteen, but only to be called a dragon in the last book of the bible revelation chapter twelve verse seven.

The good news is that God is stronger and bigger than any problem that will ever confront us in life. But this demands prevailing faith in Christ Jesus. Prevailing obstacle requires prevailing faith to overcome it. We must be determined, disciplined, dedicated and make genuine personal sacrifice and efforts.

Perhaps you have been challenged for a while with a prevailing obstacle in your life, take three minutes, and pray.

Heaven Father have mercy upon my life forgive me of my sins wash me with your blood. Reconcile me even now. Help me Lord to over come my obstacle, and short come. I thank you Jesus for your blood has prevailed for me. In Jesus mighty Name. Amen.

Chapter 2 - The Prevailing Faith

What is prevailing faith?

In these trial times that we live in, I believe strongly that there is a faith that prevails and withstand every trick and wiles of the devil.

It is written *"Put on the whole armour of God, that ye may be able to stand against the wiles of the devil"* Ephesians6:11. *"Not for that we have dominion over your faith, but are helpers of your joy: for by faith ye stand."* **2cor1:24**

"Wherefore take unto you the whole armour of God, that ye may be able to withstand in the evil day, and having done all, to stand. Stand therefore, having your loins girt about with truth, and having on the breastplate of righteousness." **Ephesians6:13-14**

In a very simple definition, prevailing faith is the faith in God that convicts us to never give up in life.

This is the overcomer's faith that prevails against every plot of the devil.

"For whatsoever is born of God overcometh the world: and this is the victory that overcometh the world, even our faith." **1John5:4.**

I encourage you today to develop prevailing faith that will not only overcome the devil but will crush every agent of the devil that was against your rising in Jesus mighty name.

This faith works with patience and hope in God.

It is written *"Cast not away therefore your confidence, which hath great recompence of reward. For ye have need of patience, that, after ye have done the will of God, ye might receive the promise."* **Hebrew10:35-36.**

As we grow in life, challenges and obstacles are bound to confront us in life.

Chapter 2 - The Prevailing Faith

We must not be ignorant of the devil wiles and schemes in life. It is written concerning the enemy; *"Be sober, be vigilant; because your adversary the devil, as a roaring lion, walketh about, seeking whom he may devour:"* **1peter5:8.**

In this trail time we live in, we need prevailing faith in God to not only withstand but to overcome the wicked one and his agents .

How do I overcome my present challenges?

It is written *"These things I have spoken unto you, that in me ye might have peace. In the world ye shall have tribulation: but be of good cheer; I have overcome the world."* **John16:33.**

It is written *"For my thoughts are not your thoughts, neither are your ways my ways, saith the Lord. For as the heavens are higher than the earth, so are my ways higher than your ways, and my thoughts than your thoughts."* **Isaiah55:8-9**

The Almighty God is sovereign and omnipotent, His ways of doing things for us is different from our ways of doing and understanding it.

Scriptures teaches us to cut our coat according to our seize. Often we over estimate and over burden our life with our own lustful desires in life. God will never give us a burden that we cannot carry.

With this in mind , I tell you that we are all above and capable to confront and over every challenge of life that the devil will ever throw at us.

"But let every man prove his own work, and then shall he have rejoicing in himself alone, and not in another. For every man shall bear his own burden" **gal6:4-5.**

We must conceive in our spirit man that God is bigger than any problem that we will ever face in life. We must remain positive and optimistic concerning every obstacle and hindrance confront our life.

Chapter 2 - The Prevailing Faith

What does this mean?

We must believe and act on God's word. Jesus said *".....blessed are they that have not seen, and yet have believed."* **John20:29.**

We must activate the word of God we hear and know according to the promises of God.

In these dielectric materialistic world that we live in today, we must always avoid lust and desire for material procession from oppressing our lives. A lot of people destroy their lives by living above their means. We cannot owe more than we own in life. We must not buy things on credit cards and pray for God to send supernatural wealth to pay it off.

We must embrace reality, humble our lives, and let God lift us up and change and increase us in life.

It is written *"The Lord is not slack concerning his promise, as some men count slackness; but is longsuffering to us-ward, not willing that any should perish, but that all should come to repentance."* **2peter3:9**

Remember….

His word is YEA … and……. AMEN..

"For all the promises of God in him are yea, and in him Amen, unto the glory of God by us." **2cor1:20.**

What are we saying?

In our life time things will happened to us that we do not have control over it. Unemployment challenges, medical and health challenges, financial short coming, helplessness, hopelessness, fear of the uncertainty e.t.c.

What we are saying is this no matter the opposition and challenges that will be fall us we must demonstrate prevailing faith in God to overcome it.

Chapter 2 - The Prevailing Faith

If prevailing circumstances remain in our lives, we must embrace prevailing faith to match up with it. We must face all opposition, contenders, and contradictions.

"What we fail to confront we cannot conquer".

"Nay, in all these things we are more than conquerors through him that loved us." **Romans8:37.**

As we progress in life the above scripture must become a reality in our life. We must face and confront all our fears and worries. We must dominate and overcome every uprising in our lives. In times of prevailing obstacles and desperate challenges we must forever have faith in God.

"Howbeit in the business of the ambassadors of the princes of Babylon, who sent unto him to enquire of the wonder that was done in the land, God left him, to try him that he might know all that was in his heart." **2chr32:31.**

Often God will search our heart to see, really our honesty and sincerity in Him. What we are saying here is that regardless of the challenges and obstacles we must engage prevailing faith to match it.

We must not give up or abandon any project we started in life.

HOW DO WE PREVAIL IN LIFE?

In life we prevail by obey the commandment of God. We prevail by practicing the written word of the Holy Scripture as a way of life.

It is written *"So mightily grew the word of God and prevailed."* **Acts19:20.**

We prevail by remaining optimistic in life. Unless we develop faith to remain optimistic in the midst of great impossibility, we will not be able to conquer and overcome it. We prevail by remain positive in the midst of calamity and prevailing harsh predicament.

Chapter 2 - The Prevailing Faith

Everyone living in disobedience of the word of God will not prevail in life. Rather the devil will inflict such persons with more trouble and frustration in their lives. In my own humbled opinion obeying Gods word is the key to a victorious life.

It is written *"If ye be willing and obedient, ye shall eat the good of the land: But if ye refuse and rebel, ye shall be devoured with the sword: for the mouth of the Lord hath spoken it."* **Isaiah1:19-20**

We prevail by the leading and presence of the Holy Spirit in our lives. Unless we develop a relationship and fellowship with the person of the Holy Spirit, we will never prevail when problem arise.

We need the Holy Ghost to be in control of our life for us to prevail against the wiles and schemes of the devil.

Therefore briefly let's examine the condition for the presence of the Holy Spirit.

CONDITIONS TO RECEIVE THE HOLY SPIRIT

REPENTANCE

Repent, and be baptized every one of you in the name of Jesus Christ for the remission of sins, and ye shall receive the gift of the Holy Ghost.

BE BAPTIZE

".... be baptized every one of you in the name of Jesus Christ for the remission of sins, and ye shall receive the gift of the Holy Ghost"

CONFESS OF YOUR SIN

If we confess our sins, he is faithful and just to forgive us our sins, and to cleanse us from all unrighteousness.

ACKNOWLEDGMENT

"Acknowledge that you are a sinner and that Jesus Christ died for your sins." **Rom3:23.**

Chapter 2 - The Prevailing Faith

BORN AGAIN

Jesus answered and said unto him, Verily, verily, I say unto thee, Except a man be born again, he cannot see the kingdom of God.

Prevailing Prayer Points

I cancel my name and that of my family from the death register, with the fire of God, in the name of Jesus.

Every weapon of destruction fashioned against me and my family, be destroyed by the fire of God, in the name of Jesus.

Power of God, fight for me in every area of my life, in Jesus' name.

Every hindrance to my breakthrough, be melted by the fire of God, in the name of Jesus.

Every hindrance to my breakthrough, be melted by the fire of God, in the name of Jesus.

Every evil power against me, be scattered by the thunder fire of God, in the name of Jesus.

Father Lord, destroy every evil man/woman in the name of Jesus.

All failures of the past, be converted to success , in Jesus' name.

O Lord, let the former rain, the latter rain and Your blessing pour down on me now.

O Lord, let all the failure mechanism of the enemy designed against my success, be frustrated, in the name of Jesus.

I receive power from on high and I paralyze all the powers of darkness that are diverting my blessings, in the name of Jesus.

Beginning from this day, I employ the services of the angels of God to open unto me every door of opportunity and breakthroughs, in the name of Jesus.

Chapter 2 - The Prevailing Faith

I will not go around in circles again, I will make progress, in the name of Jesus.

I shall not build for another to inhabit and I shall not plant for another to eat, in the name of Jesus.

I paralyse the powers of the emptier concerning my handiwork, in the name of Jesus.

Father Lord, let every locust, caterpillar and palmer-worm assigned to eat the fruit of my labour be roasted by the fire of God.

The devil shall not spoil my testimony in this programme, in the name of Jesus.

I reject every hindrance against my marriage, in the name of Jesus.

I paralyze every strongman against my life, in the name of Jesus.

Let every agent of shame fashioned to work against my life be paralyzed, in the name of Jesus.

I paralyse the activities of household wickedness over my life, in the name of Jesus.

I quench every strange fire emanating from evil tongues against me, in the name of Jesus.

Father Lord, give me power for maximum achievement

Heavenly father , give me comforting authority to achieve my goal.

I paralyse every spirit of disobedience in my life, in Jesus' name.

I refuse to disobey the voice of God, in the name of Jesus.

Every root of rebellion in my life, be uprooted, in Jesus' name.

Power of reject and regret in my life, dry up, in the name of Jesus.

Power enforcing poverty in my life, die, in Jesus' name

Chapter 2 - The Prevailing Faith

Every inspiration of witchcraft in my family, be destroyed, in the name of Jesus.

Blood of Jesus, blot out every evil mark of witchcraft in my life, in the name of Jesus.

Every garment put upon me by witchcraft, be torn to pieces, in the name of Jesus.

Angels of God, begin to pursue my household enemies, let their ways be dark and slippery, in the name of Jesus.

Lord, confuse them and turn them against themselves.

I break every evil unconscious agreement with household enemies concerning my miracles, in the name of Jesus.

Household witchcraft, fall down and die, in the name of Jesus.

Father Lord, drag all the household wickedness to the dead sea and bury them there.

My life, jump out from the cage of household wickedness, in the name of Jesus.

I command all my blessings and potentials buried by wicked household enemies to be exhumed, in the name of Jesus.

I will see the goodness of the Lord in the land of the living, in the name of Jesus.

Everything done against me to spoil my joy, receive destruction, in the name of Jesus.

O Lord, as Abraham received favour in Your eyes, let me receive Your favour, so that I can excel in every area of my life.

Lord Jesus, deal bountifully with me in this programme.

Father Lord, disgrace every power that is out to thwart Your programme for my life, in the name of Jesus.

Every step I take shall lead to outstanding success, in Jesus' name.

Chapter 2 - The Prevailing Faith

I shall prevail with man and with God in every area of my life, in the name of Jesus.

Every habitation of infirmity in my life, break to pieces, in the name of Jesus.

My body, soul and spirit, reject every evil load, in Jesus' name.

Evil foundation in my life, I pull you down today, in the mighty name of Jesus.

Every inherited sickness in my life, depart from me now, in the name of Jesus.

Every evil water in my body, get out, in the name of Jesus.

I cancel the effect of every evil dedication in my life, in the name of Jesus.

Holy Ghost fire, immunize my blood against satanic poisoning, in the name of Jesus.

Father Lord, put self control in my mouth, in the name of Jesus.

Every door open to infirmity in my life, be permanently closed today, in the name of Jesus.

Every power contenting with God in my life, be roasted, in the name of Jesus.

Every power preventing God's glory from manifesting in my life, be paralysed, in the name of Jesus.

I loose myself from the spirit of desolation, in the name of Jesus.

Glory of God, envelope every department of my life, in the name of Jesus.

The Lord that answereth by fire, be my God, in the name of Jesus.

In this programme, all my enemies shall scatter to rise no more, in the name of Jesus.

Blood of Jesus, cry against all evil gatherings arranged for my sake, in the name of Jesus.

Father Lord, convert all my past failures to unlimited victories, in the name of Jesus.

Chapter 2 - The Prevailing Faith

Lord Jesus, create room for my advancement in every area of my life.

All evil thoughts against me, Lord turn them to be good for me.

Father Lord, give evil men for my life where evil decisions have been taken against me, in the name of Jesus.

O Lord, advertise Your dumbfounding prosperity in my life.

Let the showers of dumbfounding prosperity fall in every department of my life, in the name of Jesus.

I claim all my prosperity in this programme, in the name of Jesus.

Every door of my prosperity that has been shut, be opened now, in the name of Jesus.

I stand against every evil covenant of sudden death, in the name of Jesus.

I break every conscious and unconscious evil covenant of untimely death, in the name of Jesus.

You spirit of death and hell, you have no document in my life, in the name of Jesus.

You stones of death, depart from my ways, in the name of Jesus.

O Lord, make me a voice of deliverance and blessing.

I tread upon the high places of the enemies, in the name of Jesus.

I bind and render useless, every blood sucking demon, in the name of Jesus.

You evil current of death, loose your grip over my life, in the name of Jesus.

I frustrate the decisions of the evil openers in my family, in the name of Jesus.

Fire of protection, cover my family, in the name of Jesus.

Father Lord, make my way perfect, in the name of Jesus.

I shall not be put to shame, in the name of Jesus.

Chapter 2 - The Prevailing Faith

I reject every garment of shame, in the name of Jesus.

I reject every shoe of shame, in the name of Jesus.

I reject every head-gear and cap of shame, in the name of Jesus.

Shamefulness shall not be my lot, in the name of Jesus.

Every demonic limitation of my progress as a result of shame, be removed, in the name of Jesus

Every network of shame around me, be paralysed, in the name of Jesus.

Those who seek for my shame shall die for my sake, in the name of Jesus.

No weapon fashioned against me shall ever prosper in Jesus Name.

As far as shame is concerned, I shall not record any point for satan, in the name of Jesus.

In the name of Jesus, I shall not eat the bread of sorrow in Jesus Name.

I shall not eat the bread of shame and I shall not eat the bread of defeat.

No evil will touch me throughout my life, in the name of Jesus.

In this programme, I shall reach my goal, in the name of Jesus.

In every area of my life, my enemies will not catch me, in the name of Jesus.

In every area of my life, I shall run and not grow weary, I shall walk and shall not faint.

O Lord, in every area of my life, let not my life disgrace You.

I will not be a victim of failure and I shall not bite my finger for any reason, in the name of Jesus.

Help me O Lord, to meet up with God's standard for my life.

Chapter 2 - The Prevailing Faith

I refuse to be a candidate to the spirit of amputation, in the name of Jesus.

With each day of my life, I shall move to higher ground, in the name of Jesus.

Every spirit of shame set in motion against my life, I bind you, in the name of Jesus.

Every spirit competing with my breakthroughs, be chained, in the name of Jesus.

I bind every spirit of slavery , in the name of Jesus.

In every day of my life, I disgrace all my stubborn pursuers, in the name of Jesus.

I bind, every spirit of Herod, in the name of Jesus.

Every spirit challenging my God, be disgraced, in Jesus' name.

Every Red Sea before me, be parted, in the name of Jesus.

I command every spirit of bad ending to be bound in every area of my life, in the name of Jesus.

Every spirit of Saul, be disgraced in my life, in the name of Jesus.

Every spirit of Pharaoh, be disgraced in my life, in Jesus' name.

I reject every evil invitation to backwardness, in Jesus' name.

I command every stone of hindrance in my life to be rolled away, in the name of Jesus.

Father Lord, roll away every stone of poverty from my life, in the name Jesus.

Let every stone of infertility in my marriage be rolled away, in the name of Jesus.

Let every stone of non-achievement in my life be rolled away, in the name of Jesus.

My God, roll away every stone of hardship and slavery from my life, in the name of Jesus.

Chapter 2 - The Prevailing Faith

My God, roll away every stone of failure planted in my life, my home and in my business, in the name of Jesus.

You stones of hindrance, planted at the edge of my breakthroughs, be rolled away, in the name of Jesus.

You stones of stagnancy, stationed at the border of my life, be rolled away, in the name of Jesus.

Holy Spirit, let every stone of the 'amputator' planted at the beginning of my life, at the middle of my life and at the end of my life, be rolled away, in the name of Jesus.

Father Lord, I thank You for all the stones You have rolled away, I forbid their return, in the name of Jesus.

Let the power from above come upon me, in the name of Jesus.

Father Lord, advertise Your power in every area of my life, in the name of Jesus.

Let the power to prosper throughout the days of my life fall upon me, in the name of Jesus.

Let the power to be in good health throughout the days of my life fall upon me, in the name of Jesus.

Let the power to disgrace my enemies throughout the days of my life fall upon me, in the name of Jesus.

Let the power of Christ rest upon me now, in the name of Jesus.

Let the power to bind and loose fall upon me now, in the name of Jesus.

Father Lord, let Your key of revival unlock every department of my life for Your revival fire, in the name of Jesus.

Every area of my life that is at the point of death, receive the touch of revival, in the name of Jesus.

Father Lord, send down Your fire and anointing into my life, in the name of Jesus.

Chapter 2 - The Prevailing Faith

Every uncrucified area in my life, receive the touch of fire and be crucified, in the name of Jesus.

Let the fire fall and consume all hindrances to my advancement, in the name of Jesus.

You stubborn problems in my life, receive the Holy Ghost dynamite, in the name of Jesus.

Holy Ghost fire, baptize me with prayer miracle, in Jesus' name.

Every area of my life that needs deliverance, receive the touch of fire and be delivered, in the name of Jesus.

Let my angels of blessing locate me now, in the name of Jesus.

Every satanic program of impossibility, I cancel you now, in the name of Jesus.

Every household wickedness and its program of impossibility, be paralyzed, in the name of Jesus.

No curse will land on my head, in the name of Jesus

Throughout the days of my life, I will not waste money on my health: the Lord shall be my healer, in the name of Jesus.

Throughout the days of my life, I will be in the right place at the right time.

Throughout the days of my life, I will not depart from the fire of God's protection, in the name of Jesus.

Throughout the days of my life, I will not be a candidate for incurable disease, in the name of Jesus.

Every weapon of captivity, be disgraced, in the name of Jesus.

Lord, before I finish this programme, I need an outstanding miracle in every area of my life.

Let every attack planned against the progress of my life be frustrated, in the name of Jesus.

Chapter 2 - The Prevailing Faith

I command the spirits of harassment and torment to leave me, in the name of Jesus

Lord, begin to speak soundness into my mind and being.

I reverse every witchcraft curse issued against my progress, in the name of Jesus.

I condemn all the spirits condemning me, in the name of Jesus.

Let divine accuracy come into my life and operations, in the name of Jesus.

No evil directive will manifest in my life, in the name of Jesus.

Let the plans and purposes of heaven be fulfilled in my life, in the name of Jesus.

Father Lord, do something supernatural for me in the mighty name of Jesus

Let divine strength come into my life, in the name of Jesus.

Let the power to destroy every decree of darkness operating in my life fall upon me now, in the name of Jesus.

Heavenly Father, deliver my tongue from evil silence.

Holy Spirit, let my tongue tell others of Your life.

Father Lord, loose my tongue and use it for Your glory.

Father Lord, let my tongue bring straying sheep back to the fold.

Father Lord, let my tongue strengthen those who are discouraged.

Lord, let my tongue guide the sad and the lonely.

Lord, baptise my tongue with love and fire.

Let every unrepentant and stubborn pursuers be disgraced in my life, in the name of Jesus.

Chapter 2 - The Prevailing Faith

Let every iron-like curse working against my life be broken by the blood of Jesus, in the name of Jesus.

Let every problem designed to disgrace me receive open shame, in the name of Jesus.

Let every problem anchor in my life be uprooted, in Jesus' name.

Multiple evil covenants, be broken by the blood of Jesus, in the name of Jesus.

Multiple curses, be broken by the blood of Jesus, in Jesus' name.

Everything done against me with evil padlocks, be nullified by the blood of Jesus, in the name of Jesus.

Everything done against me at any cross-roads, be nullified by the blood of Jesus, in the name of Jesus.

Let every stubborn and prayer resisting demon receive stones of fire and thunder, in the name of Jesus.

Every stubborn and prayer resisting sickness, loose your evil hold upon my life, in the name of Jesus.

Every problem associated with the dead, be smashed by the blood of Jesus, in the name of Jesus.

I recover my stolen property seven fold, in the name of Jesus.

Let every evil memory about me be erased by the blood of Jesus, in the name of Jesus.

I disallow my breakthroughs from being caged, in Jesus' name.

Let the sun of my prosperity arise and scatter every cloud of poverty, in the name of Jesus.

I decree unstoppable advancement upon my life, in Jesus' name.

I soak every day of my life in the blood of Jesus and in signs and wonders, in the name of Jesus.

Chapter 2 - The Prevailing Faith

I bind every ancestral spirit and command them to loose their hold over my life, in the name of Jesus.

Ancestral spirits, pack your loads and go out of my life, in the name of Jesus.

CHAPTER 3
THE ENDURING FAITH

"And ye shall be hated of all men for my name's sake: but he that shall endure unto the end, the same shall be saved." **Mark13:13**

In our life time, every one of us, faces problems in life. If you do not deal with them right away, even small problems can grow into giants with the potential to rule over your life.. They may not look as menacing as physical giants, but they are often just as intimidating. The good news is that God is stronger, able, bigger than every problem we will ever face in life.

Despite all the trial we face in life we must develop enduring faith to overcome every raging obstacle in life. *"But he that shall endure unto the end, the same shall be saved."* **Mathew24:13**

Chapter 3 - The Enduring Faith

Some of us have suffered for so many wrong reasons. Others have been jailed for wrong reasons, even killed for the wrong reason.

Life is built around the orbits of endurance. Does the husband have to kill himself when His pregnant wife collapse, and die with the unborn child in the labor room?

It is written *"Blessed are they which are persecuted for righteousness' sake: for theirs is the kingdom of heaven."* **Mathew5:10.**

Enduring faith requires continuous patience and learning from our own life experiences. Talking of Abraham the father of faith, it is written *"And so, after he had patiently endured, he obtained the promise."* **Hebrews6:15**.

Unless we develop patience and endurance to confront obstacles and face challenges in life, we will forever suffer defeat in life. Remember…This is the faith that encouraged and moved Joshua and Caleb to still the land. Joshua and Caleb said,

"Let us go up at once and take possession, for we are well able to overcome it"
(Numbers 13:30 NKJV).

WHY MUST I ENDURE IN LIFE?

Endurance faith is the winning and overcomers faith. One of the characteristics of people with this faith is humility and meekness. This faith is sober and diligent, always patience and content with whatever they have right now.

I am against some church folks who consider endurance as a way of life.

Chapter 3 - The Enduring Faith

It is not the will of God that we perpetually endure obstacle, child bearing, financial hardship, unemployment, and frustration in life. But often God will use patience to tame and humble us in life. Some of us are very anxious about breaking through in life. But God cannot give us what we cannot handle right now.

It is written of Abraham *"He staggered not at the promise of God through unbelief; but was strong in faith, giving glory to God; And being fully persuaded that, what he had promised, he was able also to perform."*

Romans 4:20-21.

Endurance faith is far greater challenge than our physical capability. Endurance faith operates smoothly in our heart, because it is a mental thing and not a physical thing. It is a spiritual test for God to test and weigh our attitude in life.

The heroes of faith in Hebrews 11 endured to the end, many of them not ever receiving the manifestation of the promises of God in their own lifetimes. Yet, they persevered. They endured.

The struggle for so many church folks with endurance faith is that often we cannot project or predict when God intends to fulfill His precious promises to us. One would hope to see God move in our lifetimes. Yet, many of these men and women of faith in the bible who never wavered in their commitment to serve and worship God all the days of their lives.

"By faith we understand that the universe was formed at God's command, so that what is seen was not made out of what was visible" **(Hebrews 11:3).**

Colossians 1:16-17 builds on that same thought, letting us know that all things were created by Him and for Him, that He is before all things, and in Him all things hold together.

Chapter 3 - The Enduring Faith

This is our God. Nothing is too difficult for Him. He is the all-powerful One who created the entire universe, yet He cares about you and will reward you when you earnestly seek Him. He holds the world and everything in it together, and He is willing and able to see you through any problem you will ever face.

Faith Goes Through

No one has the luxury of going through a problem-free life. The psalmist wrote, *"A righteous man may have many troubles, but the Lord delivers him from them all"* **(Psalm 34:19).**

Just knowing that God's plan is to deliver you should make it a bit easier to have an enduring faith – one that holds on to God in the time of trouble..

In Isaiah 43:1-2, God said, *"Fear not, for I have redeemed you; I have summoned you by name; you are mine. When you pass through the waters, I will be with you; and when you pass through the rivers, they will not sweep over you. When you walk through the fire, you will not be burned; the flames will not set you ablaze."*

Water and fire are sometimes used in scripture to represent calamity; water, because it overwhelms – and fire, because it consumes. Though the promises in Isaiah 43 were spoken to Israel, they also have implications for us today.

God wants you to know that no matter how overwhelming or consuming your problems may seem, He will be with you and will help you safely through to the other side.

Remember Shadrach, Meshach, and Abednego, the three Hebrew men who would not bow down to King Nebuchadnezzar's idol in Daniel 3:8-25?

Chapter 3 - The Enduring Faith

There is no doubt that God had the power to prevent these godly men from being thrown in the fiery furnace, but instead, He chose to join them in the fire.

Not only did they all survive, but we learn from Daniel 3:27 that not a single hair on their heads was singed – and they didn't even smell like smoke when they came out!

Shadrach, Meshach, and Abednego made it through the fire unscathed because they placed their enduring faith in God. They said, *"We know our God is able to deliver us...but even if He doesn't, yet will we serve Him!"* They were so steadfast in their faith that even the threat of certain death could not persuade them to give up.

Enduring Faith Demands Strong Will-power

Your faith in God will help you rise above any hardship you face. 1 John 5:4 (NKJV) says, *"...this is the victory that overcomes the world, even our faith."*

Faith overcomes, but that doesn't necessarily mean that God always immediately intervenes when we call on Him in time of need. Often God transforms our heart and the way we think by the physical experiences and challenges that will confront us in life.

This experience, provokes us develop to develop enduring faith as we continue to trust His written word and seek His face in prayers. Endurance faith in God means learning to consistently rely on God's promises rather than to give in to doubt and discouragement in life. God reward us all in life, according to the measure of our faith in him.

Despite all the frustration, assaults, and attacks the apostles and the early church father like Apostle Paul persevered some of them are not even remembered to date.

We do not have all the evidence if all of them inherited the precious promises while they were enduring and waiting in their life time.

Chapter 3 - The Enduring Faith

Just as their faith sustained them, our faith is designed to help us endure anything the devil afflicts and inflicts us with in life. Apostle Paul was forced to learn to be contend because of his enduring faith in God.

Remember.......

"Of the Jews five times received I forty stripes save one. Thrice was I beaten with rods, once was I stoned, thrice I suffered shipwreck, a night and a day I have been in the deep; In journeyings often, in perils of waters, in perils of robbers, in perils by mine own countrymen, in perils by the heathen, in perils in the city, in perils in the wilderness, in perils in the sea, in perils among false brethren; In weariness and painfulness, in watchings often, in hunger and thirst, in fastings often, in cold and nakedness."

2cor11:24-27

Enduring faith withstands trials hardship and difficulty in life.

Again recall the life of Apostle Paul, an excellent example of how enduring faith in God can help a believer endure life frustration and hardship.

He wrote, *"I have worked much harder, been in prison more frequently, been flogged more severely, and been exposed to death again and again. Five times I received from the Jews the forty lashes minus one. Three times I was beaten with rods, once I was stoned, three times I was shipwrecked. I spent a night and a day in the open sea, and I have been constantly on the move.*

I have been in danger from rivers, in danger from bandits, in danger from my own countrymen, in danger from Gentiles; in danger in the city, in danger in the country, in danger at sea; and in danger from false brothers.

Chapter 3 - The Enduring Faith

I have labored and toiled and have often gone without sleep; I have known hunger and thirst and have often gone without food; I have been cold and naked" **(2 Corinthians 11:23-27).**

Despite the revelation of the Holy Ghost , concerning what will happened to Apostle Paul, he was not only ready to go to jail but to die there also. That is enduring faith in display.

"And when he was come unto us, he took Paul's girdle, and bound his own hands and feet, and said, Thus saith the Holy Ghost, So shall the Jews at Jerusalem bind the man that owneth this girdle, and shall deliver him into the hands of the Gentiles.

And when we heard these things, both we, and they of that place, besought him not to go up to Jerusalem. Then Paul answered, What mean ye to weep and to break mine heart? for I am ready not to be bound only, but also to die at Jerusalem for the name of the Lord Jesus." **Acts21:11-13**

A through the worst of all those circumstances, Paul did not lose sight of his victory.

He even encouraged others saying, *"We are hard pressed on every side, but not crushed; perplexed, but not in despair; persecuted, but not abandoned; struck down, but not destroyed"* **(2 Corinthians 4:8-9).**

Despite all the prevailing challenges Apostle, Paul's enduring faith in God helped him to overcome all the attacks and uprising in life time.

Your enemy, the devil, wants to discourage you and make you doubt God. He does his best to convince you that your marriage will never improve, that your kids will never come back to the Lord, that you will always be sick, that you'll never have enough money, etc. Far too often, we believe the devil's lies.

Here is the truth: no problem, difficulty, or struggle that you face is bigger than God.

Chapter 3 - The Enduring Faith

In the midst of trouble, you can resist the devil, draw even closer to God and develop your faith in the One who can do the impossible! His very presence will enable you to remain strong through more than you thought possible.

Rest assured that He will not allow you to be tried beyond the strength He gives you. Just as sure as the trials come, God will provide a way out **(1 Corinthians 10:13).**

Enduring faith in God is the gateway to lasting impact in life

Do you want to make an impact in your life time?

We must develop enduring faith in God's word, practice Gods word and remain faith to God's precious promises concerning outlives.

It is written *"Faithful is he that calleth you, who also will do it."* **1teo5:24**

"There is a rare faith that pleases the heart of the Father above all others – it's called Enduring Faith. It can only be developed in the tension of having a promise from God, yet living in its lack of fulfillment.

In this place of extraordinary privilege, we have the chance to offer a sacrifice of praise and not lower the standard of God's promises to our level of experience."----**Bill Johnson**

Chapter 3 - The Enduring Faith

RELEVANT KEYS TO OVERCOME LIFE CHALLENGES

---------------------**Prayer**--------------------

We must pray about and present the matter to God.

------------------**Fellowship**-----------------

We must develop fellowship and relationship with the Holy Spirit

----------------**Believe in God**--------------

We must have confidence and believe in God

------------**Take decision in life**------------

We must take decision that is crucial and profitable to our future

CONCLUSION

Although Faith in God means believing in God to validate and make good his promise. This include us taking genuine steps in life towards actualizing our desired future and heart desire.

It is written *" Yea, a man may say, Thou hast faith, and I have works: shew me thy faith without thy works, and I will shew thee my faith by my works."* **James2:18.**

As we conclude in this book, it is time to take action in life. Perhaps you might come up with an excuse that I do not have the capital or the resources.

It is written *"For as the body without the spirit is dead, so faith without works is dead also."* **James2:26**

Really my intention is not for this book to become like a story book rather let this book preach and proclaim the message, move us into taking decisive action concerning our destinies and future.

Chapter 3 - The Enduring Faith

" Arise ye, and depart; for this is not your rest: because it is polluted, it shall destroy you, even with a sore destruction." **Micah2:10**

Nothing moves around you until we decide and take action in life. You are where you find your self today because of the previous actions you took sometimes ago. Now the standard is set … It is time to come up hitter!

" Therefore if any man be in Christ, he is a new creature: old things are passed away; behold, all things are become new. Now repeat this Prayer after me." **2cor5:17**

Say Lord Jesus, I accept you today, as my Lord and my savior, forgive me of my sins wash me with your blood. Right now, I believe, I am sanctified, I am save, I am free, I am free from the Power of sin to serve the Lord Jesus. Thank you Lord for saving me. Amen.

Congratulations: YOU ARE NOW A BORN AGAIN CHRISTIAN

AGAIN I SAY TO YOU CONGRATULATIONS

What must I do to determine my divine visitation?

To determine divine visitation you must be born again. The word says as many as received him, to them gave He power to become the sons of God. Even to them that believe on his name.

To qualify for divine visitation do the following sincerely

1) Acknowledge that you are a sinner and that He died for you. **Rom3:23**.

2) Repent of your sins. **Acts 3:19, Luke13:5, 2Peter3:9**

3) Believe in your heart that Jesus died for your sin. **Romans10:10**

4) Confess Jesus as the Lord over your life. **Romans10:10, Acts2:21**

Now repeat this Prayer after me

Chapter 3 - The Enduring Faith

Say Lord Jesus, I accept you today, as my Lord and my savior, forgive me of my sins wash me with your blood. Right now, I believe, I am sanctified, I am save, I am free, I am free from the Power of sin to serve the Lord Jesus. Thank you Lord for saving me. Amen.

Congratulations:
YOU ARE NOW A BORN AGAIN CHRISTIAN

AGAIN I SAY TO YOU CONGRATULATIONS

I adjure you to watch the Spirit of God bear witness with your Spirit confirming His word with signs following. The word says The Spirit itself beareth witness with our spirit, that we are the children of God.

Join a bible believing church or join us on our weekly and Sunday worship services at 343 Sanford Avenue Newark New Jersey 07106.

WISDOM KEYS

Every Productive Society is a society heading to the top

Millions of Nigerians run away from Nigeria, very few Nigerians stay in Nigeria.

My decision to return Nigeria is the will of God for my life

My short coming in America after 18 years, trained me to be wise, to think, reflect and reason appropriately.

If you train your mind to reason it will train your hands to earn money.

It is absurd to use the money of the heathen to build the kingdom of the living God.

Every Ministry reveals its agenda and goal either at the beginning or at the end. Be careful of your life it is your first Ministry.

The average American mind is conditioned for a continual quest to get new things and (discard the former) and throw away old things.

Chapter 3 - The Enduring Faith

When I considered well, my BMW jeep became my initial deposit for the work of the ministry in Nigeria

Everyone is waiting for you to change your mind until you change your thinking nothing changes around you.

Multiple academic degrees in other discipline gave me the chance to think, reflect and reason

What so everyone are thinking and reflecting at the moment reveals you to the time and the now factor

All events and intents are the product of precise thought processes, accurate reason every event is designed for a designated timeline

Wisdom is your ability to think, to create and invent. If you can think wise enough you will come out of penury

The distance between you and success is your creative ability to think reason and reflect accurate.

Success is the result of hard work, commitment resolve and determination learning from past mistakes and failing.

If you organize your mind you have organized your life and destiny.

There is a thin line between success and failure. If you look above and beyond you are on your way to success.

Wealth is your ability to think, power is your ability to reason and success is your ability to be informed.

If you can make use of your mind by thinking and reasoning God will make use of your life and destiny.

Think and Be Great

Reflect, Reason, think and be great

Famous people are born of woman

Chapter 3 - The Enduring Faith

That you will make it is your intention; that you will survive is your resolve, that you will succeed with changes is your determination, personal efforts and hard work.

No man was born a failure. Lack of vision is the end product of failure.

Working with mental patients encourages and aspire me to be a productive observant and dedicated to my assignment.

Successful people are not magicians, it is the will power combined with hard work, and determination and a resolve to succeed that make them succeed.

In the unequivocal state of the mind, intention is not a location or a position it is the state of the mind.

So many people think that they think. The mind is used to think reflect and reason. You will remain blind with your eye open until you can see with your mind by thinking.

There is no favoritism in accurate and precise calculation

Although knowledge is power, information is the key and gateway to a great future.

It will take the hand of God to move the hand of man.

With the backing of the great wise God, nothing will disconnect you from your inheritance.

As long as you have wisdom and understanding of God, Satan and evil cannot manipulate your life and destiny.

You have come this far by yourself judgment and decision you have made in the past, now lean and listen to God for another dimension of greatness.

Great people are common people it is extra ordinary effort and the price of sacrifice that produces greatness.

As a mental direct care worker I saw a great pastor and a motivational speaker within myself.

Menial job does not reduce your self-worth, until you resolve to achieve greatness see greatness in all you do; you will never count in your community

Chapter 3 - The Enduring Faith

The principle of Jesus will solve your gambling and addiction problems

The man of Jesus will lead you into heaven,

Everyone have their self-appraisal and what they think about you. Until you discover yourself other opinion about you will alter the real you.

Supervisors and directors are just a position in the chain of command in a work place. Never allow your supervisor hierarchy to alter your opinion about yourself.

Everyone can come out of debt if they make up their mind.

That I am not a decision maker at work does not diminish my contribution to my world.

Although it appears like it was a poor decision to accept a direct care employment at a psychiatric hospital as I reflect of my nine years of experience, it became apparent that I have learnt and experienced enough for my next assignment.

Self-encouragement and determination is a resolve of the heart.

If you are determined to make a difference, and do the things that make a difference you will eventually make a difference.

Good things do not come easy

Short cuts will cut your life short.

Those who look ahead move ahead.

Life is all about making an impact. In your life time strive to make an impact in your community.

Make friends and connect with people who are moving ahead of you in life.

If you can look around well you have come a long way in your life, made a lot of difference and realized a lot of success in life.

If you are my old friend, hurry up to reach out to me before I become a stranger to you.

Everything I am blessed with inspirations from God, that change my definition and interpretation of the world around me.

I thought I was stagnant and lonely until I looked around and noticed my children running around and my wife cooking.

Chapter 3 - The Enduring Faith

At 40 I resigned my Job to seek the Lord forever.

My ministry took a drastic rise to the top when the wisdom of God visited me with knowledge and understanding.

You will be a better person if you understand the characteristics of your personality – your mood swings attitudes and habits.

It is the seed of love you sow into the heart of a child and a woman that you reap in due time.

Love is not selfish, love share everything including the concealed secrets of the mind.

As long as you have a prayer life and a bible; you will never feel lonely, rejected and idle in the race of life.

When good friends disconnect from you, let them go, they might have seen something new in a different direction.

Confidence in yourself and in God is the only way to bring you out of captivity

Never train a child to waste his/her time.

The mind is the greatest assets of a great future.

You walk by common sense run by principles and fly by instruction.

Those who fly in flight of life fly alone.

Up in the air you are alone. No one can toll you accept the compass of knowledge and information

I have seen a tolling vehicle I have seen a tolling ship I have never seen a tolling airplane.

I exercise my judgment and make a decision every minute of the day.

Decisions are crucial, critical and vital with reference to your future.

So many people wish for a great future. You can only work towards a great future.

Your celebrity status began when you discovered your talent. What are you good at? Work at it with all commitment.

Prayers will sustain you but the wisdom of God will prosper you.

When I met Oyedepo, his teachings changed my perspective, but when I met Ibiyeomie; His teaching changed my perception.

Chapter 3 - The Enduring Faith

I will be successful in ministry if only I concentrate and focus my energy in the work of the ministry.

It took the late Dr. Vincent Pearle Norman's book to open my mind towards kingdom success.

CHAPTER 4
PRAYER OF SALVATION

I am glad you have read this book all the way from the beginning to this point. All I have said from the beginning will remain a mystery until you commit it into practice.

And before you do so I want you, if you have not given your life to Jesus to do so now. Give your life to Christ. I want you to know the truth! The truth is that Jesus died for your sins and because He died you must be alive and prosperous.

What must I do to determine my divine visitation?

To determine divine visitation you must be born again. The word says as many as received him, to them gave He power to become the sons of God. Even to them that believe on his name.

To qualify for divine visitation do the following sincerely,

Chapter 4 - Prayer of Salvation

1) Acknowledge that you are a sinner and that He died for you. **Rom3:23.**

2) Repent of your sins. **Acts 3:19, Luke13:5, 2Peter3:9**

3) Believe in your heart that Jesus died for your sin. **Romans10:10**

4) Confess Jesus as the Lord over your life. **Romans10:10, Acts2:21**

Now repeat this Prayer after me

Say Lord Jesus, I accept you today, as my Lord and my savior, forgive me of my sins wash me with your blood. Right now, I believe, I am sanctified, I am save, I am free, I am free from the Power of sin to serve the Lord Jesus. Thank you Lord for saving me. Amen.

Congratulation:
YOU ARE NOW A BORN AGAIN CHRISTIAN

AGAIN I SAY TO YOU CONGRATULATION

I adjure you to watch the Spirit of God bear witness with your Spirit confirming His word with signs following. The word says The Spirit itself beareth witness with our spirit, that we are the children of God.

MIRACLE CARE OUTREACH

"...But that the members should have the same care one for another" **1cor12:25**

We are all members of the body of Christ. Jesus commanded us to love our neighbor as ourselves. This includes caring for one another as a member of one body. True love is expressed in caring and giving. The word says for God so Love He gave....

Reach out to someone in need of Jesus, help someone in crisis find Christ. Look out and prove your love to Jesus by caring and inviting your friends and associates to find Jesus the Healer.

Chapter 4 - Prayer of Salvation

Invite your friends to our Home Care Cell Fellowship (Miracle chapel Intl Satellite fellowship) In the USA at 33 Schley Street Newark New Jersey 07112.

If you are in Nigeria—**MIRACLE OF GOD MINISTRIES**

A.K.A "MIRACLE CHAPEL INTL" Mpama –Egbu-Owerri Imo state Nigeria.

(Home Care Cell fellowship Group). We meet every Tuesday at 6:00pm-7:00pm.

LIFE IS NOT ALL ABOUT DURATION BUT ITS ALL ABOUT DONATION

What does the above statement mean?....

"Life consists not in accumulation of material wealth.." **Luke12:15.**

"But it's all about liberality....meaning- what you can give and share with others." **Proverb11:25.**

When you live for others--You live forever- because you out live your generation by the legacy you live behind after you depart into glory to be with the Lord. But when you live to yourself - you are reduced to self—you are easily forgotten when you die and depart in glory.

Permit me to admonish you today to live your life to be a blessing to a soul connected to you today. I want you to know that so many souls are connected and looking up to you, and through you so many souls will be saved and rescued from destruction. Will you disciple someone today to find Jesus Christ?

"As a genuine Christian; it is your duty to evangelize Jesus Christ to all you meet on your way. Jesus is still in the healing business-Jesus is still doing miracles from time of old to now.

Therefore tell someone about Jesus Christ today, disciple and bring them to Church."

John 1:45 Philip findeth Nathanael....

Please to prove the sincerity of your love for God today; please become a soul winner. The dignity of your Christianity is hidden in your boldness to proclaim and evangelize Jesus Christ to all you meet on your way.

There is a question mark on the integrity of your Christianity until you become a life soul winner. Invite someone to join us worship the Lord Jesus this coming Sunday.

Amen

MIRACLE OF GOD MINISTRIES

PILLARS OF THE COMMISSION

We Believe Preach and Practice the following,

1) We believe and preach Salvation to every living human being

2) We believe and preach Repentance and forgiveness of sins

3) We believe and preach the baptism of the Holy Spirit and Spiritual gifts

4) We believe and teach the Prosperity

5) We believe and preach Divine Healing and Miracles (Signs &Wonder)

6) We believe and preach Faith

7) We believe and Proclaim the Power of God (Supernatural)

8) We believe and Proclaim Praise& Worship to God

9) We believe and preach Wisdom

10) We believe and preach Holiness (Consecration)

11) We believe and preach Vision

12) We believe and teach the Word of God

13) We believe and teach Success

14) We believe and practice Prayer

15) We believe and teach Deliverance

This 15 stones form the Pillars of Our Commission.

Become part of this church family and follow this great move of God.

MY HEART FELT PRAYER FOR YOU

It is my burning desire for God to touch you through one of our teaching books, cd's. It also my personal desire for you encounter God for yourself.

Now let me Pray for you:

O Lord God! I beseech thee, and through personal prayer intercession today that the Holy Spirit will touch this precious soul reading this book and turn their life around. Spirit of God possess this loved one. Lord overcome all dominating controlling forces that has prevailed over their lives.

I come against all oppressive though in Jesus Name. Henceforth; I pronounce you free, from manipulation, intimidation and domination of the wicked enemy called the devil. You are free from all satanic harassment and assaults. **Amen**

TIME TO TURN TO GOD

"I like you all to know today, that God is Spirit." **John4:24**

"God is not a man that He should lie." **Number23:19.**

"Now God searches into the heart." **Jer29:13.**

Chapter 4 - Prayer of Salvation

Until you repent genuinely, you will never be able to please Him. Until you develop supernatural faith as a lifestyle you will not be able to please God.

God told Samuel... *"But the Lord said unto Samuel, Look not on his countenance, or on the height of his stature; because I have refused him: for the Lord seeth not as man seeth; for man looketh on the outward appearance, but the Lord looketh on the heart."* **1samuel16:7**

It is my prayer for you to consciously seek the face of the Lord forever more. If you have never accepted Jesus Christ as your savior we can do it right here in this small book.

Just say Lord Jesus

CHAPTER 5
ABOUT THE AUTHOR

Rev Franklin N Abazie is the founding and Presiding Pastor of Miracle of God Ministries with headquarters in Newark, New Jersey USA and a branch church in Owerri- Imo State Nigeria. He is following the footsteps of one of his mentors, Oral Roberts (Healing Evangelist) of the blessed memory.

The Lord passed Oral Roberts healing mantle two days before he went to be with the Lord at age 91 into the hand of healing evangelist-Rev Franklin N Abazie in a vision.

In all his services the Power and Presence of God is present to heal all in his audience. He is an ordained man of God with a Healing Ministry reviving the healing and miracle ministry of Jesus Christ of Nazareth.

Chapter 5 - About the Author

Pastor Franklin N Abazie, is called by God with a unique mandate:

"THE MOMENT IS DUE TO IMPACT YOUR WORLD THROUGH THE REVIVAL OF THE HEALING & MIRACLE MINISTRY OF JESUS CHRIST OF NAZARETH
I AM SENDING YOU TO RESTORE HEALTH UNTO THEE AND I WILL HEAL THEE OF THY WOUNDS. SAID THE LORD OF HOST"

He is a gifted ardent Teacher of the word of God who operates also in the office of a Prophet, generating and attracting undeniable signs & wonders, special miracles and healings, with apostolic fireworks of the Holy Ghost.

He is the founding and presiding senior Pastor of this fast growing Healing ministry.

He has written over 86 inspirational, healing and transforming books covering almost all aspect of divine healing and life. He is happily married and blessed with children.

BOOKS BY REV FRANKLIN N ABAZIE

1) Commanding Abundance
2) The outcome of faith
3) Understanding the secret of prevailing prayers
4) Understanding the secret of the man God uses
5) Activating my due Season
6) Overcoming Divine Verdicts
7) The Outcome of Divine Wisdom
8) Understanding God's Restoration Mandate
9) Walking in the Victory and Authority of the truth
10) Gods Covenant Exemption
11) Destiny Restoration Pillars
12) Provoking Acceptable Praise
13) Understanding Divine Judgment
14) Activating Angelic Re-enforcement
15) Provoking Un-Merited Favor
16) The Benefits of the Speaking faith
17) Understanding Divine Arrangement

18) Understanding Divine Healing
19) The Mystery of Endurance
20) Obeying Divine Instructions
21) Understanding the Voice of God
22) Never give up on Hope
23) The prevailing Power of faith
24) Understanding Divine Prosperity
25) The Reward of Prayer
26) Covenant Keys to Answered Prayers
27) Activating the Forces of Vengeance
28) Put your faith to work
29) Where is your trust?
30) The Audacity of the Blood of Jesus
31) Redeeming Your Days
32) The force of Vision
33) Breaking the shackles of Family Curses
34) Wisdom for Marriage Stability
35) The winners Faith
36) The Prayer solution
37) The power of Prayer
38) Prayer strategy
39) The prayer that works
40) Walking in Forgiveness
41) The power of the grace of God

42) The power of Persistence
43) Overcoming Divine verdicts
44) The audacity of the blood of Jesus.
45) The prevailing power of the blood of Jesus
46) The benefit of the speaking faith.
47) Fearless faith
48) Redeeming Your Days.
49) The Supernatural Power of Prophecy
50) The companionship of the Holy Spirit
51) Understanding Divine Judgement
52) Understanding Divine Prosperity
53) Dominating Controlling Forces
54) The winners Faith
55) Destiny Restoration Pillars
56) Developing Spiritual Muscles
57) Inexplicable faith
58) The lifestyle of Prayer
59) Developing a positive attitude in life.
60) The mystery of Divine supply
61) Encounter with God's Power
62) Walking in love
63) Praying in the Spirit
64) How to provoke your testimony

65) Walking in the reality of the Anointing
66) The reality of new birth
67) The price of freedom
68) The Supernatural power of faith
69) The Power of Persistence
70) The intellectual components of Redemption
71) Overcoming Fear
72) The Force of Vision
73) Overcoming Prevailing Challenges
74) The Power of the Grace of God
75) My life & Ministry
76) The Mystery of Praise

MIRACLE OF GOD MINISTRIES
NIGERIA CRUSADE 2012

MIRACLE OF GOD MINISTRIES
NIGERIA CRUSADE 2012

MIRACLE OF GOD MINISTRIES

NIGERIA CRUSADE

2012

MIRACLE OF GOD MINISTRIES

NIGERIA CRUSADE

2012

www.ingramcontent.com/pod-product-compliance
Lightning Source LLC
Chambersburg PA
CBHW021153080526
44588CB00008B/313